Jazz Styles
Level Four

Supplement to All Piano and Keyboard Methods
Compiled and Edited by Wesley Schaum

Foreword

Jazz styles, evolving over many years, encompass a broad range including ragtime, blues, boogie, swing and rock. A casual, improvisational attitude is the common thread. The syncopated rhythms and harmonies have remained popular for many generations and provide fascinating educational material.

This collection includes arrangements of authentic ragtime by Scott Joplin and Charles I. Johnson as well as original works by Stanford King, Lavoy Miller Leach, Wesley Schaum and Ladonna J. Weston.

Index

Exclusively Distributed By

HAL•LEONARD®
CORPORATION
7777 W. BLUEMOUND RD. P.O. BOX 13819 MILWAUKEE, WI 53213

Maple Leaf Rag

Scott Joplin
Arr. by Wesley Schaum

Energico ♩ = 116-132

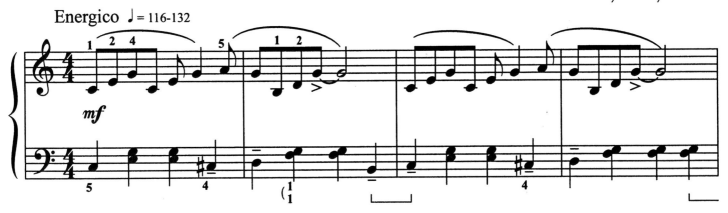

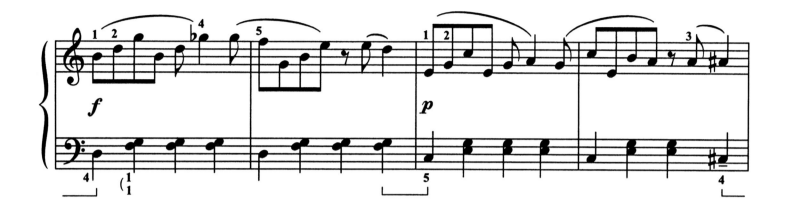

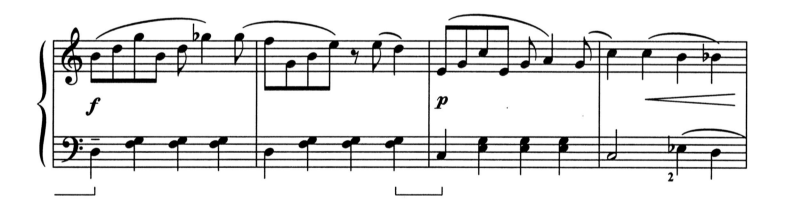

Solid Sound

Wesley Schaum

Con anima *(swing 8ths) ♩ = 152-168

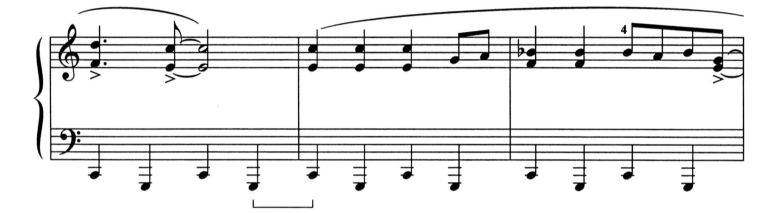

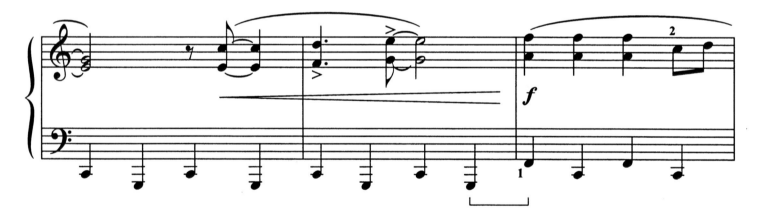

* Swing 8th notes are played in a modified triplet style:

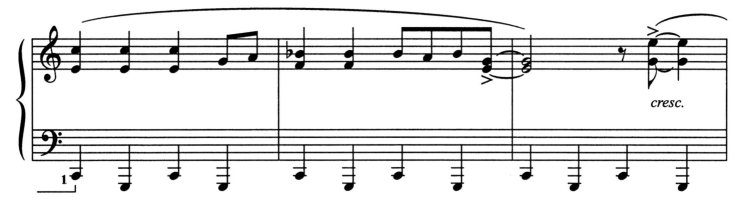

cresc.

ff

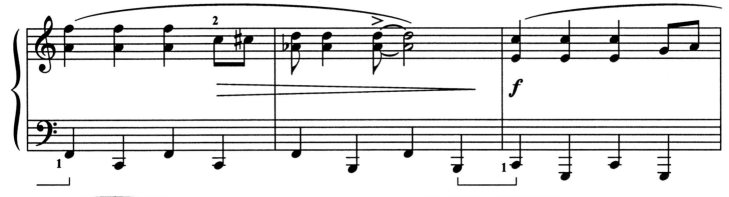

f

mf

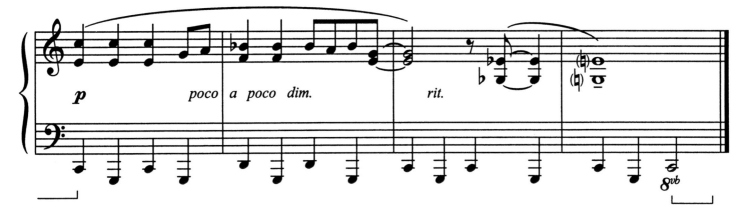

p   poco a poco dim.   rit.

Feelin' Moody

Wesley Schaum

Andantino ♩ = 96 - 108

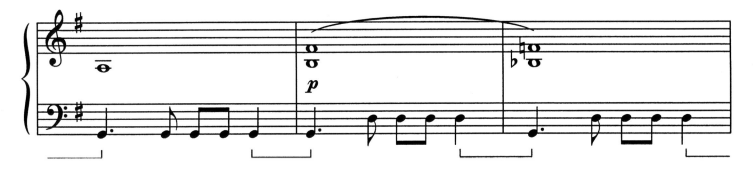

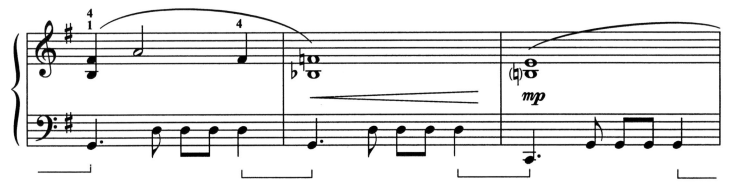

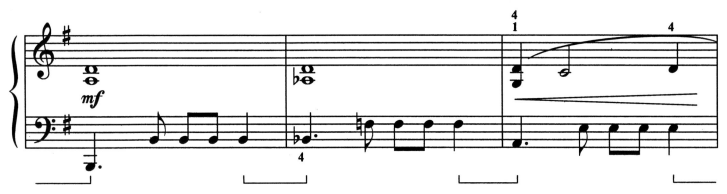

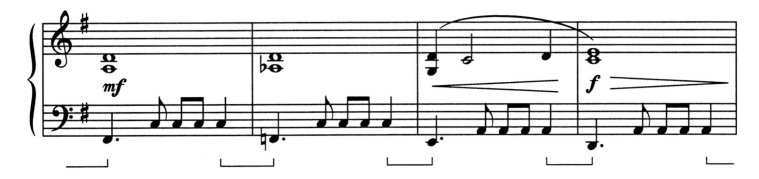

Square Bear

Wesley Schaum

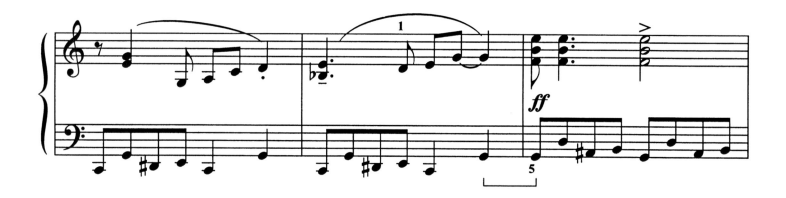

Little Swinger

Wesley Schaum

Vivace (swing 8ths) ♩ = 152-168

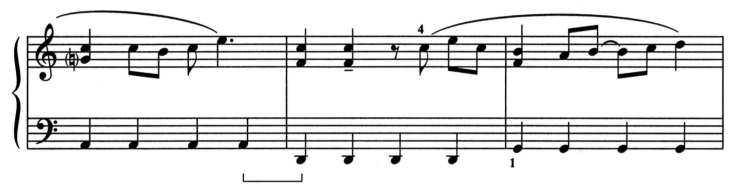

Original Rags

Scott Joplin
Arr. by Wesley Schaum

Giocoso ♩ = 126 -138

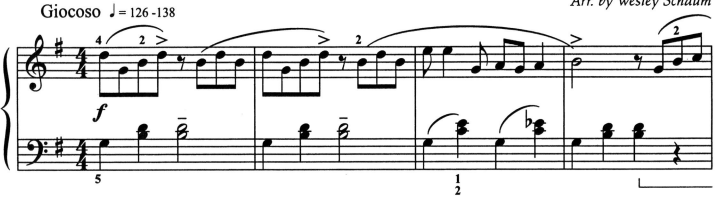

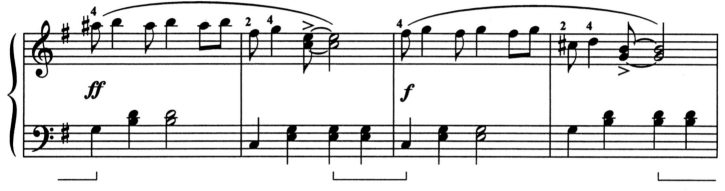

Miz Tuttle Shuffle

Lavoy Miller Leach

Allegretto (swing 8ths) ♩= 120-138

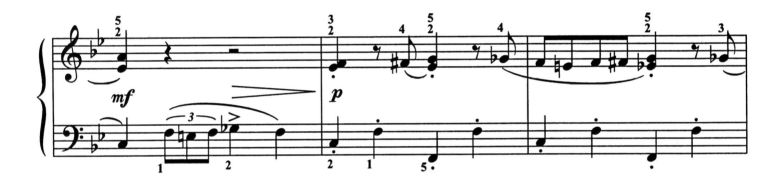

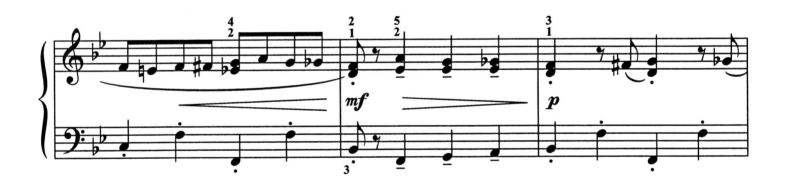

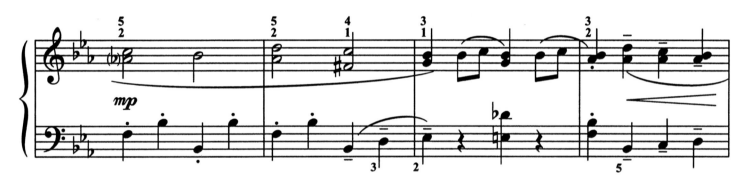

Ramblin' Swing

Stanford King

Vivo (swing 8ths) ♩ = 116-132

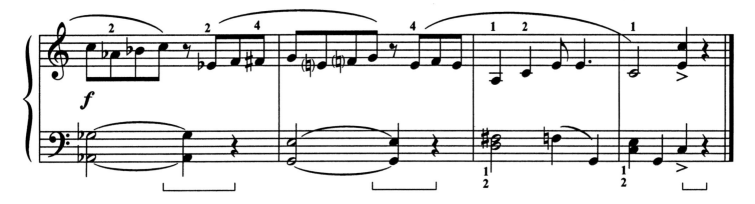

Sure Fire

Wesley Schaum

All Right

Wesley Schaum

Animato (swing 8ths) ♩ = 126-144

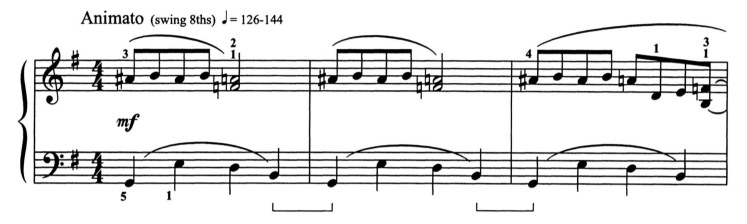

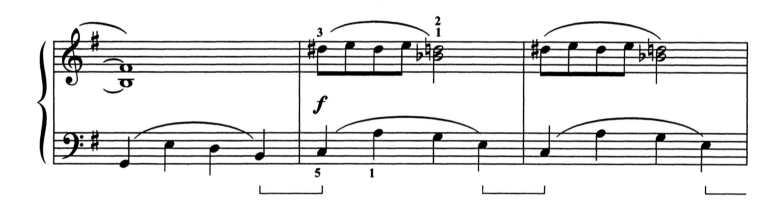

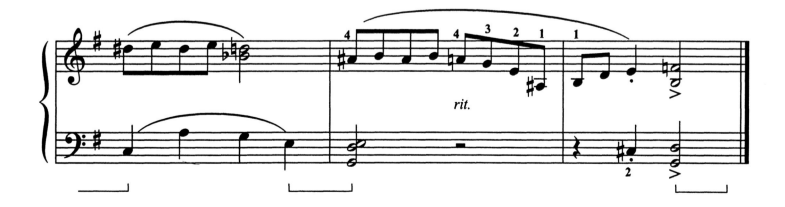

Big City Rag

Charles I. Johnson
Adapted by Wesley Schaum

Allegretto ♩ = 120-138

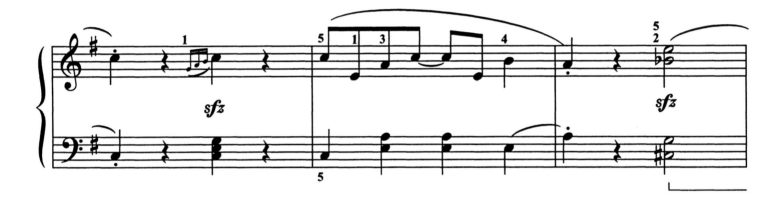

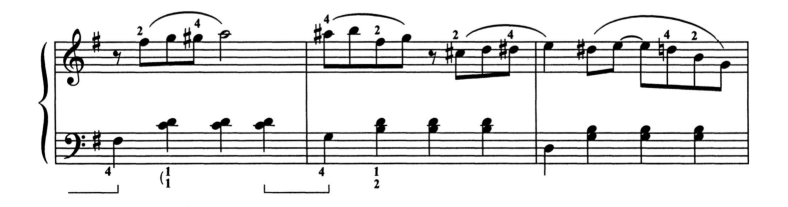

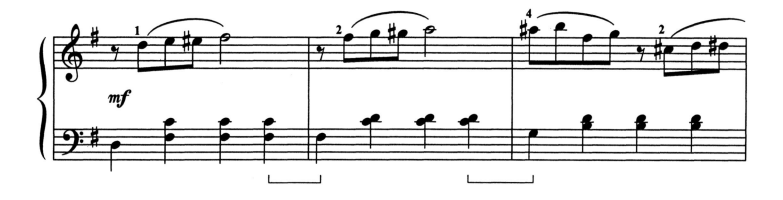

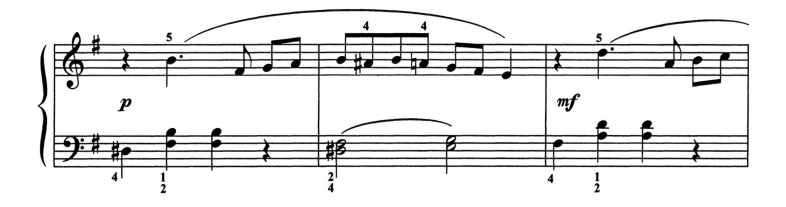

Pure Blue

Wesley Schaum

Moderato ♩ = 100-112

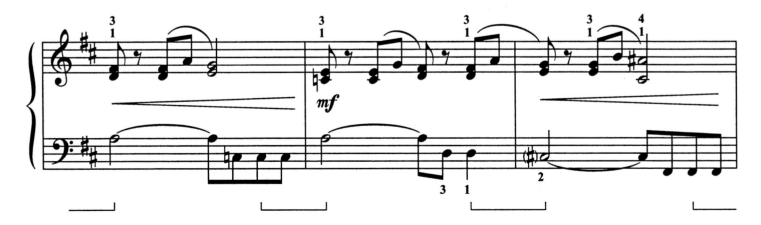

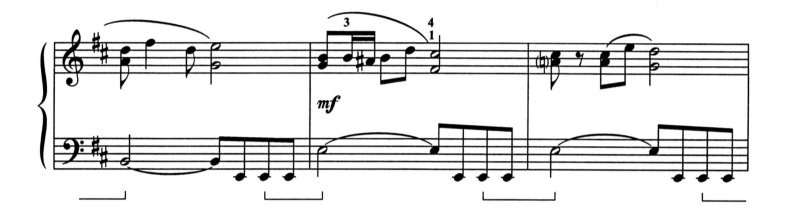

Horsin' Around

Ladonna J. Weston

Moderato (swing 8ths) ♩ = 112-126

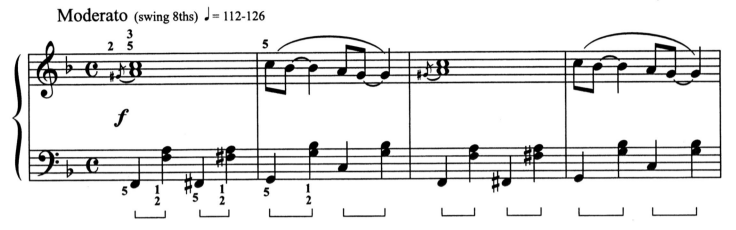

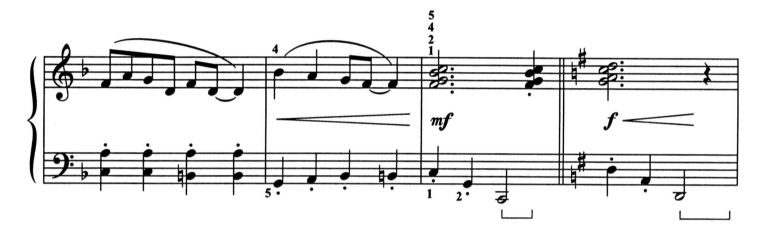

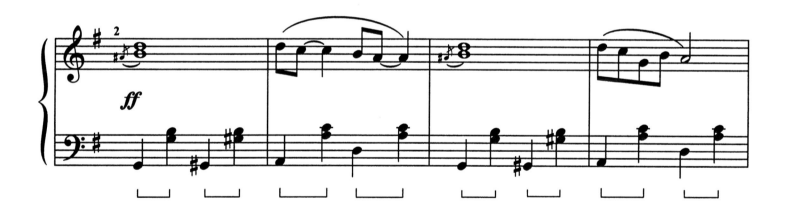

Rhythm Workbook

- **NEW Music Engraving with Improved Note Spacing makes Better Visual Recognition of Note Values**
- **Helps Increase Rhythmic Understanding**
- **Counting-and-Clapping Drills Emphasize Rhythmic Feeling**
- **For Students of All Ages**

PRIMER LEVEL

(02-21)

Use from the Very First Lesson

- Helps develop undestanding and feeling for fundamental rhythms
- Step-by-step presentation correlated with rhythm drills and time signatures
- Very gradual and thorough

LEVEL ONE

(02-22)

Adding Missing Rests
Correlating Rests and Notes
Measure Bar Placement • Ties and Slurs
Multiple 8th Notes • Note Alignment
Rest and Note Value Names
2/4, 3/4 and 4/4 Time Signatures

LEVEL TWO

(02-23)

Natural Accents • Upbeat Notes
Single 8th Notes and Rests
6/8 and 3/8 Time Signatures
16th Notes in Various Time Signatures
Staccato and Extension Dots
Syncopation • Ties and Slurs

LEVEL THREE

(02-24)

Accents • Basic Grace Notes • Cut Time
Dotted Rests • Divided Accompaniment
Dotted 8th and 16th • Fermata (hold)
Melody Divided Between Hands
Rolled Chords • Trills • Tempo Marks • Triplets

LEVEL FOUR

(02-25)

- Teaches an understanding and feeling for rhythms
- Clear explanations and helpful illustrations
- Includes swing 8th notes, dotted rests, main counts, syncopated patterns, 3/2 and 12/8 time

Primer Level:

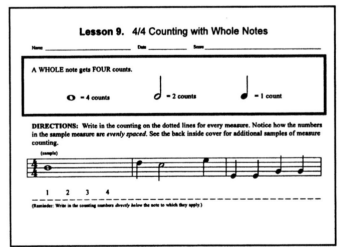

Level Two:

Theory Workbook

- *Trains Eyes to Read Intervals, Note Groups and Rhythms*
- *Helps Improve Speed and Accuracy of Note Reading*
- *Written Assignments are Reinforced with Keyboard Work*
- *Clear Explanations Save Lesson Time*

Primer Level (02-80)

Use from the Very First Lesson

- Eye Training: Up, Down and Repeated Note Motion
- Features Interval Reading of White Key 2nds, 3rds, 4ths and 5ths Up and Down in Bass and Treble

Includes: Note and Rest Values
Key Signatures
C, F and G Major Triads

Level One (02-81)

- Continues Eye Training to Recognize Intervals and other Note Groups.

Includes: Scale Construction • Basic Leger Lines
Transposing by Scale Degree • Slurs and Ties
Tempo Marks • Stem Placement • Major Triads

Level Two (02-82)

- Eye Recognition of Repeated Notes in Adjoining Intervals and Chords
- More Leger Lines • Intervals • Transposing
- Adds Accent Marks • Syncopation • 16th Notes
Pedal Marks • Clef Changes • Chromatic Scales

Level Three (02-83)

- Emphasizes Recognition of Broken Chords
Accompaniment Patterns • Melody Patterns
- Eye Recognition beyond One Measure at a Time
Reading Music Analytically • Triplets • Trills
Dotted 8th+16th • Metronome • Grace Notes

Level Four (02-84)

- Eye Recognition and Ear Training involving
Major and Minor Triads • Syncopated Rhythms
Major and Harmonic Minor Scales

Includes: Relative Minor • Phrasing
Transposing by Interval • 6th and 7th Chords
1st and 2nd Inversions of Triads

Primer Level:

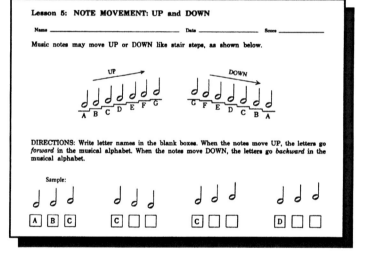

Level One:

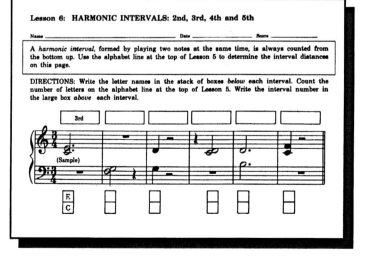

Successful Schaum Sheet Music

This is a Partial List — Showing Level 4 through Level 5

• = Original Form   ✓ = Chord Symbols

Level Four